All Together

PROGRAM AUTHORS

James A. Banks
Kevin P. Colleary
Linda Greenow
Walter C. Parker
Emily M. Schell
Dinah Zike

CONTRIBUTORS

Raymond C. Jones
Irma M. Olmedo

Macmillan/McGraw-Hill

Geography

RFB&D
learning through listening

Students with print disabilities may be eligible to obtain an accessible, audio version of the pupil edition of this textbook. Please call Recording for the Blind & Dyslexic at 1-800-221-4792 for complete information.

The McGraw-Hill Companies

Macmillan McGraw-Hill

MHID 0-02-153362-8   ISBN 978-0-02-153362-6   Printed in the United States of America

2 3 4 5 6 7 8 9 10   058/043   13 12 11 10 09

All Together
Table of Contents

Unit 2 All About Earth

EXPLORE The Big Idea **How do we learn about where we live?** 1

Skills and Features

Maps

Unit 2

How do we learn about where we live?

Find out more about where we live at www.macmillanmh.com

All About Earth

People, Places, and Events

Jenny

Jenny and her family
live in Indiana.

For more about People, Places, and Events, visit
www.macmillanmh.com

Indiana Dunes

The **Indiana Dunes National Lakeshore** is on the shore of Lake Michigan.

Duneland Harvest Festival

Jenny enjoys folk music during the **Duneland Harvest Festival**.

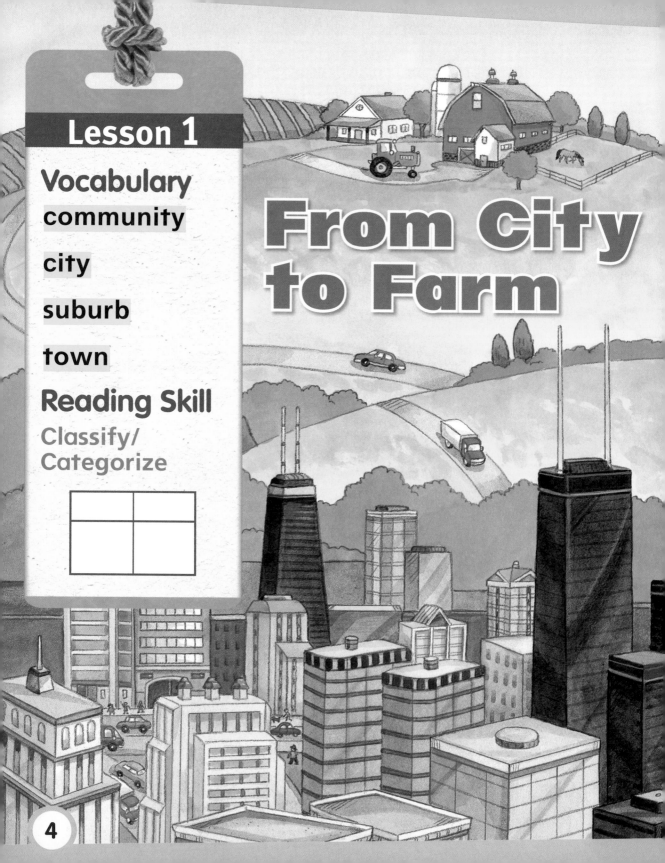

Lesson 1

Vocabulary

community

city

suburb

town

Reading Skill

Classify/
Categorize

From City to Farm

A City

A **community** is a place where people live, work, and have fun together. Welcome to the **city** of Chicago! A city is a big and busy community where many people work and live.

In a city you might live in a tall building. You could look down and see people and cars on the street below.

 What is special about a city?

Chicago

Suburbs and Towns

Welcome to Brookfield, a **suburb** of Chicago, Illinois. A suburb is a community located near a city.

In Brookfield, you might live in a house. You could play in your backyard with your friends. You might also play in a big park.

Chicago

Brookfield

Many people live in Brookfield but work in Chicago. They might take a bus, train, or car to work every day.

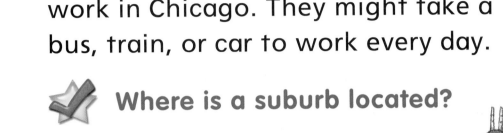 **Where is a suburb located?**

Places
Plainfield, Indiana

Plainfield is a suburb near Indianapolis. If you lived in Plainfield, you could take a short car trip to visit the Children's Museum of Indianapolis.

Towns and Farms

Danville is a **town** in Indiana. A town is much smaller than a city. It is smaller than most suburbs, too. Farms are located near towns like Danville.

If you lived on a farm, you could have lots of open space. Your family might grow food, like corn or tomatoes. You might help feed the cows and horses.

On days off from school, you could go to the nearest town with your family. You could shop or see a movie.

 What is it like to live on a farm?

Check Understanding

1. **Vocabulary** What is a **city**?

2. **Classify/Categorize** What things might you see in a city? On a farm?

3. Why do you think it is noisier in a city than in a town?

Vocabulary

transportation

diagram

Reading Skill

Classify/
Categorize

People Change the Land

Changing the Land

Homes are built every day. Often, workers have to cut down trees and smooth out the land.

Sometimes builders have to change the way the water flows! It takes a lot of work to make a community.

 How do workers build homes?

Moving from Place to Place

The way people move from place to place is called **transportation**. People drive cars, trucks, and buses on the roads and over bridges. They ride trains over the train tracks. They fly across the sky in airplanes, too!

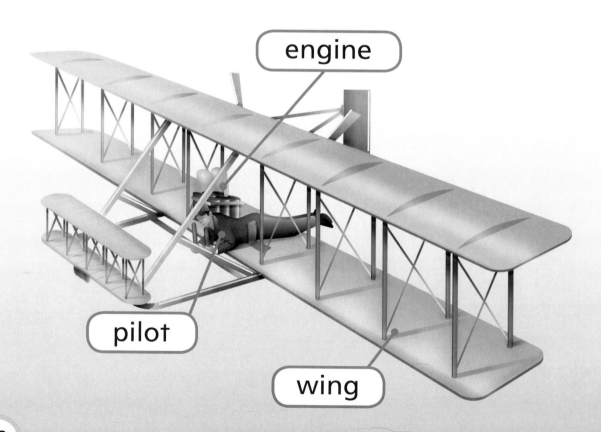

engine

pilot

wing

Look at the **diagram** on page 12. A diagram shows the parts of something. This diagram shows the first airplane. It was built by the Wright brothers over 100 years ago.

 What is transportation?

Check Understanding

1. **Vocabulary** What does a **diagram** show?

2. **Classify/Categorize** How do people travel?

3. **EXPLORE The Big Idea** Why do people make roads, bridges, and train tracks?

Looking at Earth

Vocabulary

Earth

mountain

plain

hill

ocean

river

lake

Reading Skill

Classify/
Categorize

Land and Water

We live in different communities. We live in cities, suburbs, towns, and farms. But we all live together on **Earth**.

Earth is our home. Earth is made up of land and water.

 What is Earth made of?

land

water

mountain

Different Kinds of Land

A **mountain** is the highest kind of land on Earth. Take a hike with your family in the Black Mountains of North Carolina!

A **plain** is a large, flat area of land. Go for a run across the plains of South Dakota. Watch out for the bison!

plain

hill

A **hill** is smaller than a mountain, but higher than a plain. Look at the beautiful flowers as you hike across the hills of Washington.

 What are plains?

Around the World

Rita lives in Italy near the Alps. The Alps are mountains. Italy also has hills and plains.

Water All Around

There is more water than land on Earth. The largest body of water is called an **ocean**. Take a swim in the Atlantic Ocean on a New Jersey beach.

A **river** is a long stream of water that flows into a larger body of water. Ride a raft on the Colorado River in Arizona.

river

ocean

A **lake** is a body of water with land all around it. Catch a walleye fish in Swamp Lake in Minnesota.

lake

 What is a river?

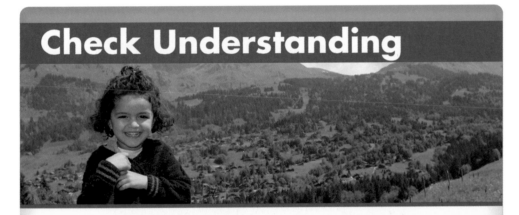

Check Understanding

1. **Vocabulary** What is an **ocean**?

2. **Classify/Categorize** What kinds of land and water can you name?

3. What kinds of land and water are near your home?

Use Globes and Maps

Vocabulary

globe

map

Look at this **globe**. It is a model of Earth. You can spin a globe to see every part of Earth. Earth is round.

A **map** is a drawing of a place. Look at the map on the next page. This map shows all of Earth on one flat paper.

Earth

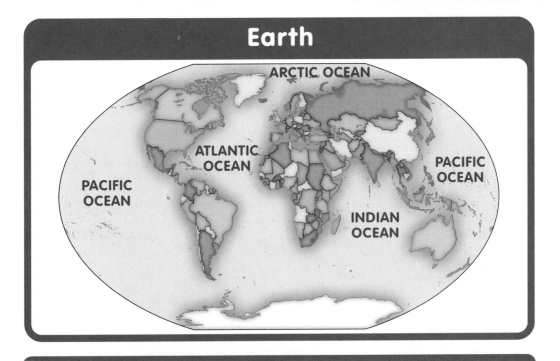

ARCTIC OCEAN

ATLANTIC OCEAN

PACIFIC OCEAN

PACIFIC OCEAN

INDIAN OCEAN

Try the Skill

1. What is a **globe**?

2. How is a map different from a globe?

Writing Activity Find an ocean on a globe. Write its name. Now find the same ocean on a map.

Learning about Earth

Lesson 4

Vocabulary

weather

season

natural resource

recycle

Reading Skill

Classify/ Categorize

Weather

What did you wear to school today? Does your answer have something to do with **weather**? Weather is how hot, cold, wet, or dry it is outside.

In Barrow, Alaska, it is snowing. At the same time, it might be sunny at your house!

 What is weather?

summer

fall

Seasons

In some places, the weather changes with the **seasons**. A season is one of the four parts of the year. The four seasons are summer, fall, winter, and spring.

In the summer it is hot in many places. Leaves drop from trees in the fall. In the winter it can be snowy and cold. In the spring, new plants grow.

winter

spring

 Can you name the four seasons?

Event
Winter Lights Festival

The Winter Lights Festival is held each year in Valparaiso, Indiana. The festival ends with fireworks!

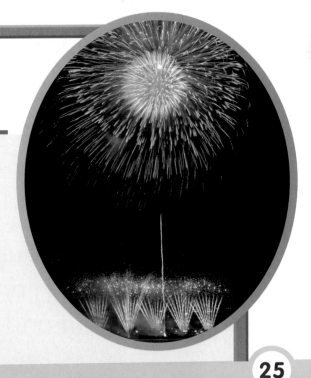

air water soil sun

Caring About Earth

Air, water, soil, and the sun are all natural resources. A **natural resource** is something in nature that we use.

We take care of natural resources when we **recycle**. Recycle means to change a thing into something new and useful.

We can recycle our newspapers into new paper. We can use our bottles and jars again and again.

We can use less water, too. If we use less water now, we will still have water years from now.

 How can you take care of natural resources?

Check Understanding

1. **Vocabulary** What are **natural resources**?

2. **Classify/Categorize** What kinds of things can you do in winter? In summer?

3. How do the seasons change where you live?

Citizenship

Democracy in Action

Respecting Earth

To respect means to treat as important. We show respect for Earth by keeping it clean.

Please stop! Do not make someone else pick up your trash!

Joe saw Emily dropping her trash.
He helped Emily respect Earth.
What would you do?

Lesson 5

Vocabulary

state

country

continent

Reading Skill

Classify/
Categorize

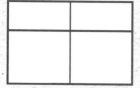

Our World

Our State and Our Country

A **state** is one part of a country.
A **country** is a land and the people
who live there.

Our country is called the United States
of America. We have 50 states in
our country.

 **How many states are
in our country?**

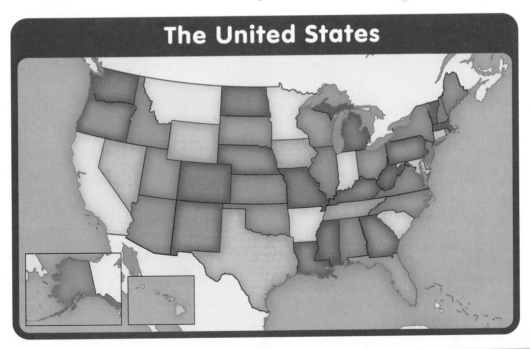

The United States

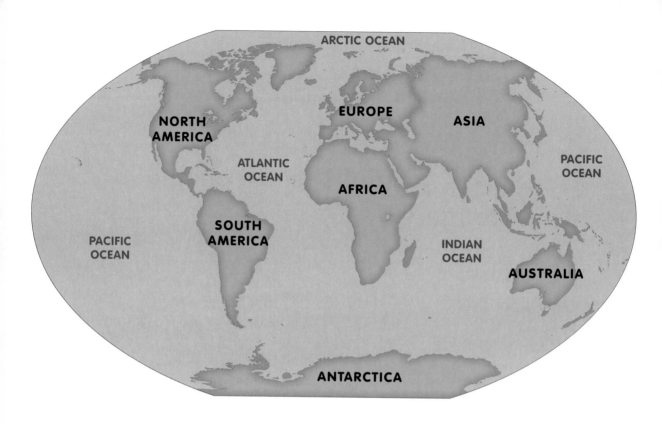

Our Continent

There are seven large areas of land on Earth. They are called **continents**. We live on the continent of North America. The seven continents are separated by four oceans. Can you find North America?

 Can you name the four oceans?

People

Ellen Ochoa, Astronaut

Ellen was the first Hispanic American woman to fly in the space shuttle. She said, "I never got tired of watching the Earth . . . as we passed over it."

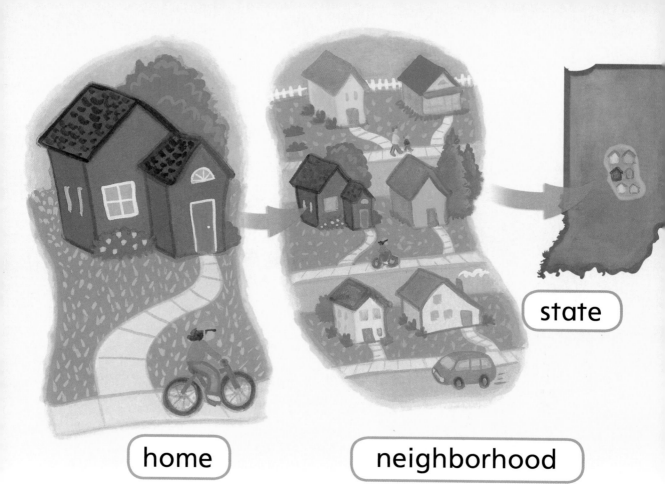

state

home

neighborhood

Where You Live

You belong to many places. There are many ways to name the places where you live.

 Where in the world do you live?

34

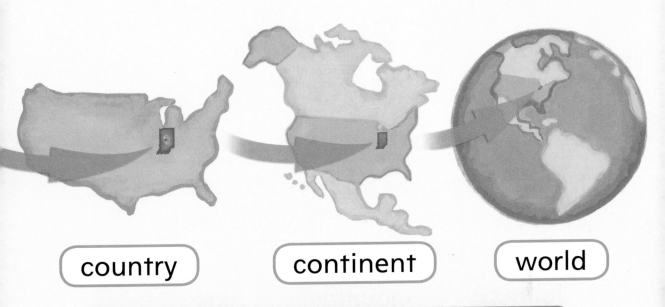

country   continent   world

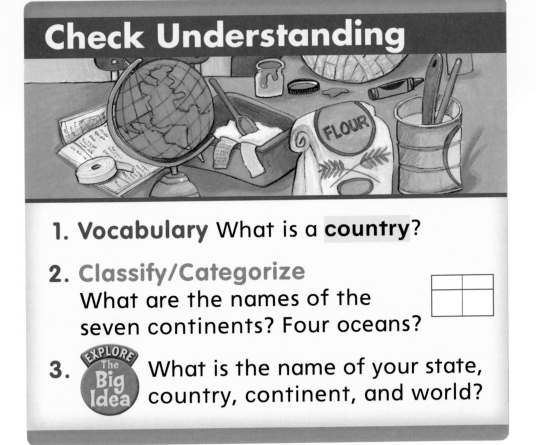

Check Understanding

1. **Vocabulary** What is a **country**?

2. **Classify/Categorize**
   What are the names of the
   seven continents? Four oceans?

3. **EXPLORE The Big Idea** What is the name of your state,
   country, continent, and world?

Review and Assess

Vocabulary

Number a paper from 1 to 3. Next to each number write the word that matches the meaning.

suburb   **mountain**   **lake**

1. an area located near a city

2. a body of water with land all around it

3. the highest kind of land

Critical Thinking

4. What are some ways that you use water?

5. Why do people change the land?

Skill

Use Globes and Maps

Look at the map of Earth. Answer the question below.

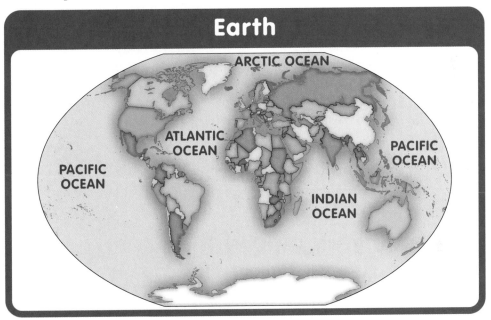

Earth

ARCTIC OCEAN

ATLANTIC OCEAN

PACIFIC OCEAN

PACIFIC OCEAN

INDIAN OCEAN

6. What parts of Earth are blue on the globe and on the map?

A. continents

B. oceans

C. countries

Geography Activity

Make a Playground Map

1 Draw a map of your playground.

2 Add symbols for the slide, swings, and more.

3 Give your map a title.

4 Share your map with the class.

Picture Glossary

C

city A **city** is a big and busy place where many people work and live. (page 5)

community A **community** is a place where people live, work, and have fun together. (page 5)

continent A **continent** is one of the seven large areas of land on Earth. (page 32)

country A **country** is a land and the people who live there. (page 31)

D

diagram A **diagram** is a picture that shows the parts of something. (page 13)

E

Earth **Earth** is our home. It is made of land and water. (page 15)

G

globe A **globe** is a model of Earth. (page 20)

H

hill A **hill** is smaller than a mountain, but higher than a plain. (page 17)

L

lake A **lake** is a body of water with land all around it. (page 19)

M

map A **map** is a drawing of a place. (page 20)

mountain A **mountain** is the highest kind of land. (page 16)

N

natural resource A **natural resource** is something in nature that we use. (page 26)

air   water   soil   sun

O

ocean An **ocean** is the largest body of water. (page 18)

P

plain A **plain** is a large, flat area of land. (page 16)

R

recycle **Recycle** means to change a thing into something new and useful. (page 26)

river A **river** is a long stream of water that flows into a larger body of water. (page 18)

S

season A **season** is one of the four parts of the year. They are summer, fall, winter, and spring. (page 24)

state A **state** is one part of a country. (page 31)

The United States

suburb A **suburb** is a place located near a city. (page 6)

T

town A **town** is a place where people live and work. It is smaller than a city. (page 8)

transportation **Transportation** is the way people move from place to place. (page 12)

W

weather **Weather** is how hot, cold, wet, or dry it is outside. (page 23)

Index

This index lists many things you can find in your book. It tells the page numbers on which they are found. If you see the letter *m* before a page number, you will find a map on that page.

Index

Credits

Maps: XNR

Illustrations: 4: Linda Howard Bittner. 6-7 Linda Howard Bittner. 8: Linda Howard Bittner. 9: Linda Howard Bittner. 12: Argosy. 24-25: Alessia Girasole. 26: Alessia Girasole. 30: Deborah Melmon. 33: Deborah Melmon. 34-35: April Hartman

Photography Credits: All Photographs are by Macmillan/McGraw-hill (MMH) except as noted below.

COV (br) Ariel Skelley/Blend Images/CORBIS, (bl) Super-Stock, (t) Comstock/SuperStock; i Ariel Skelley/Blend Images/CORBIS; 1 Kevin Schafer/CORBIS; 2 BananaStock/PunchStock; 3 (b) AP Photo/Bloomington Herald-Times; (t) David Muench/CORBIS; 5 Mark Segal/Getty Images; 6 Danita Delimont/Alamy Images; 7 Jim Baron/Image Finders; 9 Mark Segal/Getty Images; 10 Lester Lefkowitz/Getty Images; 11 (l) David Frazier PhotoLibrary,(r) David Frazier PhotoLibrary; 13 Lester Lefkowitz/Getty Images; 14 Kevin Anthony Horgan/Getty Images; 15 SUNNYpho-tography.com/Alamy Images; 16 (b) Jake Rahs/Getty Images, (t) David Muench/CORBIS; 17 (b) Prisma/Super-Stock, (t) Robert Glusic/Getty Images; 18 (c) Michael Melford/Getty Images; 18-19 (b) Jean-Pierre Pieuchot/Getty Images; 19 (c) Prisma/Superstock, (t) Layne Ken-nedy/CORBIS; 20 Michelle D. Bridwell/PhotoEdit; 22 Alaska Stock; 23 Ariel Skelley/Blend Images/Jupiterim-ages; 25 Stouffer Productions/Animals Animals; 27 (b) Ariel Skelley/Blend Images/Jupiterimages, (t) Ariel Skel-ley/Getty Images; 28 (bc) Photowood Inc./Alamy Images, (bl) Ken Karp for MMH; 29 (bkgd) Photowood Inc./Alamy Images, (c) Ken Karp for MMH; 33 National Aeronautics and Space Administration; 37 Michelle D. Bridwell/Pho-toEdit; 38 (b) Macmillan McGraw-Hill, (t) C Squared Stu-dios/Getty Images; R1 Mark Segal/Getty Images; R2 (bc) Layne Kennedy/CORBIS, (c) Robert Glusic/Getty Images, (tc) Michelle D. Bridwell/PhotoEdit; R3 (b) Ariel Skel-ley/Getty Images, (bc) Jake Rajs/Getty Images, (c) Jean-Pierre Pieuchot/Getty Images, (t) David Muench/CORBIS; R4 (bc) Jim Baron/Image Finders, (t) Michael Melford/Getty Images; BKCOV Comstock/SuperStock.